The Optometrist

by Jenny Giles
Photography by Glenn Reynolds

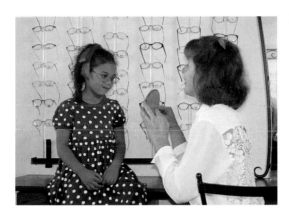

NELSON PRICE MILBURN

I am going to the optometrist.
I can't see very well,
and she is going to look
at my eyes.

Dad is coming with me.

We are in the waiting room.
We look at all the frames.

Some of the frames are little.
They are for children like me.

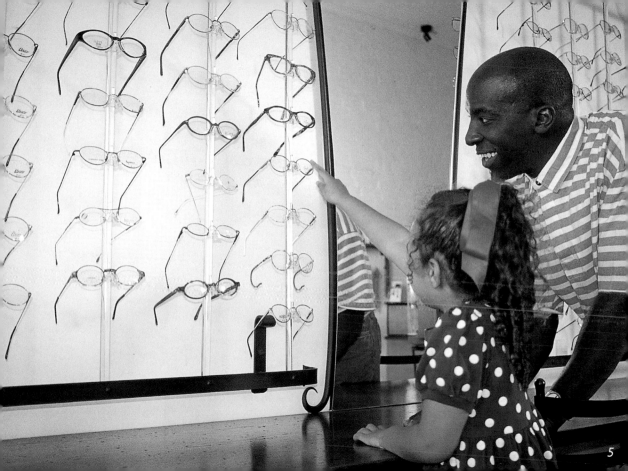

We go into a room
with the optometrist.

She talks to me,
and I talk to her.

I sit up on the chair.

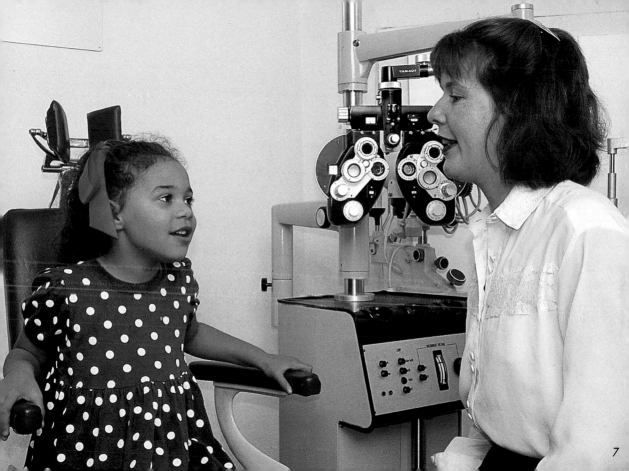

The optometrist has a card with some letters on it.
The letters at the top are big, and I can read them.
I can't see the little letters very well.

R H D V U		
P N Z R D	13	
H P V F U	10	
N E H U P	8	
Z N V E F	6·3	
E D F Z R	5	
N Z H D E	4	
Z U V E H	3·2	
R V F U P	2·5	
E P N H U	2	
U F R D N	1·6	
Z D P R F	1·3	

The optometrist

has a little light.

She looks into my eyes with it.

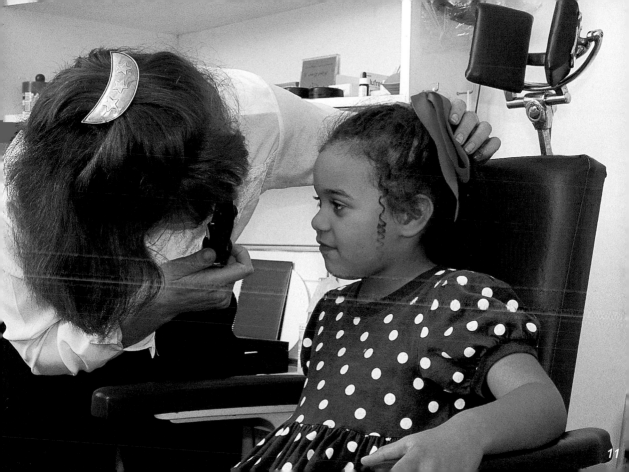

The optometrist
puts some glasses on me,
and I look at the letters again.
I can see the little letters now!

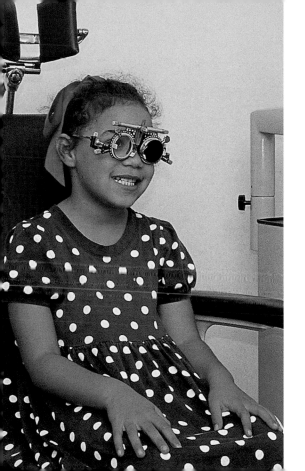

I read the letters with one eye.
Then I read them with my other eye.

I am going to get some glasses.

We go back to the waiting room,
and I see some little frames
that I like.
Dad says they look good on me.

I wave goodbye,
and we go home.
I will get my glasses next week.